THE WORD AT HOME

DR. DERRICK L. RANDOLPH, SR.

THE WORD AT HOME

Table of Contents

A little about me and My Call to Teach

I was introduced to the church as a child and exposed to powerful preaching, prayer, praise and worship. I witnessed the power of God at work both in the church and in the home as I watched my great aunts and uncles call the family together for prayer. At church, I witnessed hours of praise and worship each week. I did not know God for myself then (as a child). I was formally introduced to Jesus Christ in my mid-twenties outside of a recording studio in downtown Baltimore, Maryland. God transformed me from a local hip hop artist into a disciple.

After a few years of developing faith, I had an honest and sincere conversation with God that I will never forget. When I finally realized that I needed God, I got on my knees to pray. My mind wandered to other people, places and things. Then I asked God why I lost focus when I tried to pray. God spoke to me for the first time and clearly said "Keep your mind on me and you will have peace. Never take your mind off of me. If you do, you will never be happy!" In that moment I had a deeply spiritual experience that was instrumental in my faith walk. It is also one of the moments I return to when I consider how far God has brought me. A year later God told me that He had something else for me to do. I am glad that I followed Him.

Now that I am liberated and living this new life in Christ, I have experienced both highs and lows, as well as unexpected turns along the journey. What I find interesting in my life is how the path of parenthood provided some unique experiences that helped me develop my faith in God. I remember watching my infant son suffer a very near death experience in the NICU right before my eyes. In that moment, my wife and I could only watch, pray and hope that God would intervene for us.

God showed up a minute after my son should have died and spared his life. I also watched his twin brother overcome a rare and unnamed blood disorder. The doctor could not explain it, but we knew God delivered them both. In both cases, I was armed with only my faith in Jesus Christ to help me overcome the feelings of hopelessness and despair.

Now, there have been many trials that have challenged my family's faith in God. There were times where hope and prayer did not bring instant deliverance. Instead, I had to learn to endure. I've since learned that faith requires long-term dependence upon God to sustain it.

What's unique about our faith is that it calls you and steers you in directions that you would not typically choose. Early on, I sensed the call to return to high school to help the young people avoid the mistakes I made. I found myself teaching math in a neighborhood that I grew up in. Years later, I sensed the call to serve the next generation of young people in ministry. This seemed suitable for me, as I was a former school teacher and YMCA sports camp instructor. God led me to the children's ministry at my local church where I would use my experience on the journey to help nurture our children. I was in a season of waiting on God, and while waiting, it was a blessing turning my attention toward our children, and discovering how we would teach them.

My Assignment

One year, I was assigned a classroom with a large mural that portrayed beautiful images representing various biblical stories. I was challenged to teach the New Testament stories of the Bible. This challenge became apropos because I was about to implement my doctoral project. I started by identifying each picture's biblical story. Then I built a three question catechism to teach the lessons of each story.

We (teachers) asked the children to read each story and answer the basic, but most relevant question of the story from a child's point of view. For the second question, we asked a basic question about the theological topic (or theme) of each story. The third question dealt with the application of the main point. There was always a scripture that helped the child apply the main point of the story.

I called it the Foundation of faith catechism. It was based on fifteen biblical stories, and the three catechism questions and answers, (e.g. the relevant question, a theological question and an applicative question). To create the relevant question, I conducted an exegesis of the text. The exegetical process also helped me arrive at the appropriate answer. The second question asks about the theological theme being discussed in the text, e.g. faith, salvation, love, etc. I incorporated the traditional Baptist doctrine used by my local church to provide the foundation of the answer. The third question simply asks how to apply the core teaching of the story in everyday life. The answer was a scriptural reference that also serves as a suitable memory verse. The catechism was the foundation for the curriculum that I taught in my classroom. Each lesson in the curriculum included the catechism and an activities to meet each of the audio, visual, tactile and kinesthetic learning styles of the children.

In the end I discovered that when children read the Bible, they were able to draw conclusions on the stories to answer relevant questions. Unfortunately, they did not have knowledge of any theological concepts (or themes) like who is God, if God was created, etc. Lastly, the children were able to easily look up the scriptures and remember them. Time will tell if they would learn to apply the scriptural lessons in their lives.

Based on the children's journal entries, I discovered that the children enjoyed reading stories in the Bible. They were moved by the miracles performed by Jesus. They were drawn to the human element in the divine-human interactions and felt connected with the human emotions experienced in the stories, like sadness and pain. When I talked with them, I discovered that many of the children are committed to the spiritual disciplines, e.g. praying. They are very active in church. They have active prayer lives at home and at church, though in some children there appeared to be only occasional Bible reading at home. That's where we will begin the discussion, on the urgent need to teach the Word at Home. My hope is to provide the church with a resource that will engage, enlighten, inspire, educate and edify the church's leaders, educators and parents on how we can implement Christian Education at home.

My Discoveries

Now that I've shared my call to teach and my challenge to produce a children's curriculum, what follows are my research based discoveries. Outlined below are the topics you will read about.

My discoveries were birthed out of my research on the catechism. I concluded that there is an urgent need to teach our children. In fact, it is more urgent than I thought.

1. First, I discovered that the catechism is still useful for addressing the urgent need to teach our children. The need is more urgent than I thought and the catechism is more useful than I suspected.
2. Secondly, I discovered that God commanded parents to teach their children while the parents are still growing in Christ themselves.
3. Then I discovered that the early theologians focused on the family.
4. Lastly, I discovered the core theological teachings that we must understand and then teach.

Finally, I will introduce the Journey of Faith Model for understanding our individual development in the faith. I recommend it for building a collaborative relationship between the church and parents, as we disciple our children. I truly believe we can build a better bond between the church and the family. We can lay a firm foundation of faith in our children, and if we work together, we can help get the Word at Home.

God Bless you!

Discovery #1 - The Catechism is Still Useful

I was exploring new concepts and looking for resources to build a children's curriculum when I was referred to a common form of teaching called the catechism. After doing a little bit of research, I discovered that it was a form of "oral instruction"[i] presented as questions and answers. It piqued my interest. It was based on "rote response", repetition, constant questioning where you are teaching the answers until the students learn both question and answer.

Catechisms have been used since the church's early history and they're still used today to provide a summary of "religious doctrine."[ii] Catechizing comes from the "Late Latin word catechizare, and the Greek word katēchein, which literally means to dig into,"[iii] from "*kata*- cata- + *ēchein* which means to resound."[iv] It allows the teacher "to impress by insistent repetition"[v] information into the learner over and over. This teaching style is useful if you want to "hammer words into someone"[vi] and produce in the learner the capacity to echo what's been taught.

I felt that I could use the catechism to teach basic biblical truths and theological concepts. I realized that it could be useful for a variety of ministries, e.g. as a component of the children or youth's curriculum, an introduction to new members' education, or as a reinforcement method in a doctrinal based Bible study. I chose to use it to develop a foundation of faith in children, to empower them for the journey many of them were beginning to encounter. For the children, it would be a new way to tell the old story. They could retell the stories of our faith back to us in small pieces. One day, they would tell it to the world!

Let's look at the catechisms through the years

Catechisms in the Early Church

As technology advances and new methods of teaching are explored, former methods of teaching, like the catechism are unearthed and brought back into the conversation. The catechism seemed to address the immediate need for a training method and it can be aligned with any local church's doctrine, theological posture, or spiritual direction. I took a historical look into the works of Martin Luther, John Wesley and several contemporary scholars to determine how they addressed the need for consistent, coherent instruction. I wondered, if we could use it to instill an informed understanding of God, God's expectations, and their duties as Christians. Here's what I discovered.

Catechisms were used in the Jewish synagogue and the Christian church to prepare people for membership. They were taught in the oldest theological school, where Clement and Origen taught.

In the fourth century, Cyril of Alexandria's Catechetical Lectures were a standard work in the Greek Church. In the fifth century, at the request of a deacon, Augustine wrote a famous book on catechizing (De catechizandis rudibus), and a brief exposition of the Creed and the Lord's Prayer (Enchiridion) to show teachers what was deemed necessary for the instruction of Christians. In the Middle Ages the monks Kero (720) and Notker (912), both of St. Gall, Otfrid of Weissenburg (870), and others prepared catechetical manuals or primers of the simplest kind. The first Protestant catechisms were prepared by Lonicer (1523), Melanchthon (1524), Brentius (1527), Althamer, Lachmann (1528), and later by Urbanus Rhegius.[vii]

Catechisms in the Middle Church Era

Sixteenth century German theologian, and author of the ninety-five theses, Martin Luther, contributed a noteworthy catechism during the Reformation. Here's why. Luther visited the churches in the state of Saxony, Germany in 1528-29. After this visit, he felt the "laity was ignorant and the clergy was unfit to teach them."[viii] Luther was compelled to write the Small Catechism to help "families instruct the young and uneducated" (Krych, 4).[ix] Luther believed the catechism would help them acquire "the minimum knowledge required of a Christian." He wrote the Large Catechism later that year "for pastors, teachers, and adult laity" (Krych, 4).[x] Luther found ways to help the church leaders become responsible for teaching, the members responsible for learning, and for the next generation responsible for the future of the church.

According to Church Historian Philip Schaff, the catechisms were developed in reverse order. "The Large Catechism developed into a continuous exposition instead of a set of questions and answers that was deemed not suitable for children; therefore in July, 1529, he wrote a shorter, more practical, Little Catechism called Enchiridion, which was introduced into public schools, churches, and families and became a sort of layman's Bible for German people" (Schaff).[xi] Schaff speaks of how Luther masterfully adapted "the mysteries of the kingdom of heaven to the capacity of children." During the sixteenth century, the Reformation influenced other writers that produced catechisms. A few works are still useful, e.g. Luther's Little Catechism (1529). When compared, their teachings on religious instruction commonly include the articles of the Apostles' Creed, the Ten Commandments, and the Lord's Prayer.

Two centuries later, John Wesley developed a catechism for children that he titled *Instructions for Children*. Wesley believed preachers should assume a leadership role in religious education by teaching the catechism, and distribute it to parents who should also teach it. Wesley believed it "was one of three books that should be supplied to every Methodist society and in every house, serving as the chief textbook for the religious education of children in Methodist homes."[xii] The intent of Wesley's instruction was not merely that the Methodists would become more knowledgeable in their doctrinal beliefs, but that they would grow in holiness of heart and life.[xiii]

John Wesley wrote the Instructions for Children on December 26, 1776 in Wesley's Works, Volume XIII to eighteenth century parents and teachers in England to help them form the faith and behaviors of Christians of all ages. He conceded that the catechism in use at that time "was not appropriate for children ages six and seven,"[xiv] therefore he wrote the Instructions for Children. Liberty University cofounder, Elmer Towns adds an important observation, that "the work begun by parents should be continued in the schools by instructors."[xv]

Wesley's desire to instruct young children was perhaps fueled by his strong belief that children were ready for salvation and for spiritual formation. When questioned whether Wesley had a right to instruct children and to train others to do so, Wesley answered, "Neither had St. Paul, nor any of the apostles. What then? Were they, therefore, unable to instruct parents? Not so. They were able to instruct everyone that had a soul to be saved."[xvi] In fact, Wesley "never considered a child as a child, but rather as a unit for salvation, bred in sin, and apt to evil, but able to have a genuine and deeply religious life."[xvii]

Catechisms in Modern Times

In recent scholarship, there has been much discussion about the source of Wesley's influence for focusing on the education of children. Elmer Towns attributes it to Wesley's mother, "Susanna Wesley, who raised ten children at the Epworth Rectory. Though she valued the education they would receive from her, her principle intention was to save their souls."[xviii] Body believes Wesley "was influenced by the Dutch educator, Comenius and that when Wesley visited Jena and Herrnhut in Germany, he saw the practical application of Comenius' teaching in action. For, Comenius taught a series of principles that stems from the belief that whatever is to be known can be taught,"[xix] even to children.

The Catholic Church also left an imprint on the development of the catechism, by introducing catechisms to Colonial America in the eighteenth century. By the 1820s, Catholics opened Sunday schools where priests, seminarians, nuns, and laypersons taught the children (Reid). In the 1930s, the Confraternity of Christian Doctrine (CCD), a Vatican-inspired movement, brought a renewed effort to reach out to the children. According to New Testament author Daniel Reid, by the 1960s, when Catholic schools declined significantly, a new emphasis was placed on educating adults. Schools offered "a means of reaching children by informing their parents."[xx] The Catholics believed that catechesis can make a person's "faith become living, conscious, and active, through the light of instruction."[xxi] Each generation put the catechism to good use.

Can we build a Modern Catechism

I would like to propose the question, can we create modern catechisms today? According to Lutheran Theological Seminary professor Margaret Krych, the problem of "widespread biblical illiteracy"[xxii] created the need for serious theological learning.[xxiii] As a result, "a considerable number of catechisms have been published." When assessing the need for contemporary teaching resources, it is worth recalling the 1784 Conference of the Methodist Episcopal Church in America. It asked: *What shall we do for the rising generation?* In response, preachers were asked to meet with their society's children in groups of ten, for one hour a week. They were to "procure our instructions for them, and let all who can, read and commit them to memory." In the 1856 Methodist Episcopal Church Doctrine and Disciplines book, the catechesis became a shared obligation between clergy, lay teachers, and parents.[xxiv] The church invited lay teachers and parents to catechize children.

There has always been a need to teach the children, and a need for resources. "Early Christian literature provided few resources on family and care of children."[xxv] The adversary has always attempted to thwart the spiritual formation in children. Early on, "this was evident even in the Passion of Perpetua and Felicity; where an account is given of a group martyrdom at Carthage in A.D. 203. Then persecution was directed against conversion to Christianity and the teachers and catechists who promoted it."[xxvi] Today, the conversion of children must become a priority and we must ensure we have resources to help them grow.

Again, can we build a catechism that is beneficial to the children and useful for parents? What can we teach children to prepare them for a spiritual life of faithfulness to God? Should it be as simple as Luther's? Should it be based on the Ten Commandments like the common protestant catechisms of the eighteenth through twentieth centuries? Will it prepare the children for salvation, as Wesley would want? Should it teach about the person and character of God? How about the qualifications for living for Christ? Should we limit it to biblical texts? Should we use contemporary interpretations and modern scholarship, provided by today's thinkers?

Tennessee Wesleyan College professor, Dr. William McDonald asked "what might a simple curriculum look like, perhaps, the prison letters of Dietrich Bonhoeffer or Nelson Mandela? Could it explore the life and witness of forbears like Saint Francis of Assisi, Teresa of Avila, and Sojourner Truth? Should it include the thoughts of Abraham Joshua Heschel, or Reinhold Niebuhr, the "Letter from the Birmingham City Jail, or the "I Have a Dream" speech? The possibilities are endless both for the young and for the continuing education of adults.

The possibilities for a modern catechism are enhanced, of course, by the creativity of our pastors and the use of film, animation, the internet, television, travel and the life and faith present in so many of our congregations" (McDonald, 14).[xxvii] McDonald challenged me to ask myself if we are neglecting the experiences, stories, lessons, and wisdom of our past. How can we pass down the teachings of the modern heroes of our faith? How can we pass down the lessons long gleaned from applying biblical teachings to the trials we face in our communities every day? I ask and urge my readers to explore how to modernize the content of our teaching.

Discovery #2 - There's a Command to Teach At Home

So far, we've learned that teachers and parents use rote question and answering to pass down Christian and cultural lessons to the next generation. Now, let's look at the biblical command to teach our children. There is a unique yet foundational requirement for providing the spiritual formation in children that's found in the Old Testament book of Deuteronomy. First, here is a little about Deuteronomy.

The book of Deuteronomy concludes the five-volume set of books called the Pentateuch, which is often referred to as the Law of Moses. The Jews usually call it "sēper hattôrâ, which means 'the book of the law,'[xxviii] authored by Moses, "the divine law giver."[xxix] The Greek translation for Deuteronomy is "the second law, a repetition of God's commandments,"[xxx] a restatement of the law given at Sinai that was "originally recorded in Exodus, Leviticus, and Numbers."[xxxi]

Deuteronomy "presents itself as a mosaic of speeches given by Moses to Israel before crossing the Jordan River and entering the Promised Land (Dt 1:1)."[xxxii] These speeches are also seen as a "series of four sermons, summarizing the history and laws of Israel."[xxxiii] While Deuteronomy recapitulates the chronicles of Israel, it is also a magnificent portrait of God's loving providence. It has "high religious value as it speaks to the unity, supremacy and goodness of God."[xxxiv] Deuteronomy's retelling of the Decalogue and commission to obedience has provided fruitful instruction for generations.

The Lord is your God

Deuteronomy 6:4-9 reads, "Hear, O Israel: The Lord is our God, the Lord alone. You shall love the Lord your God with all your heart, and with all your soul, and with all your might. Keep these words that I am commanding you today in your heart. Recite them to your children and talk about them when you are at home and when you are away, when you lie down and when you rise. Bind them as a sign on your hand, fix them as an emblem on your forehead, and write them on the doorposts of your house and on your gates" (NRSV).

Let's walk through the landscape of Deuteronomy as Moses prepares the Israelites for the journey. "Deuteronomy [chapters] 1-3, cover the sojourn from Sinai to Jordan. In chapters 4-5, Moses gives an "exhortation to obey the commands of God, to teach the children to shun idolatry. Moses is teaching that safety and prosperity depend on loyalty and obedience to God."[xxxv] Biblical scholars believe the Deuteronomy 6:4-9 text is presented in the "literary form of a treaty between God and Israel, similar to the second millennium BC political treaty given to the Hittites."[xxxvi] This is Moses' farewell, being delivered to the Israelites to prepare them to enter into a relationship with God.

In our text, Moses has left Mt. Sinai. He is leading the Hebrew children to the Promised Land. As they reach the border of the Promised Land, God takes a moment to remind them of something He already taught them at Mt. Sinai. It was a warning ahead of time. Sometimes God has to stop us along the way and give us a pep talk ahead of time, before He moves us on to the next chapter in our lives. It's similar to how parents of small children stop and give them a little talk before going in to the store, or before going to a family member's house. Sometimes God needs to remind us of who we are ahead of time.

In Deuteronomy 6:4, Moses gathers everyone together and tells them "Hear, O Israel: The Lord is our God, the Lord alone. Now that word, "Hear" is important. It is "the imperative form of the first word, "Hear!" is "Shema.""[xxxvii] As a result, verse four is referred to as the Schema. The Shema is probably the "best brief, practical guide that parents have for communicating the faith to [their] children."[xxxviii] "It is in the front rank of biblical statements about God and what God expects of parents. The Shema was so important to the Hebrews that they recited it when they woke up in the morning to remind them of God and how they were to conduct family life during the day. When they went to bed at night, they repeated it again in order to judge how well they lived up to its requirements."[xxxix]

In the Shema, we find "the emblematic declaration that Yahweh is Israel's God and Yahweh is one [is] made in verse four and then exposited in verses five through nine."[xl] Moses stops them to say 'Hear this!' You might not understand it, believe it, or want to hear it, but the absolute truth is that "Yahweh" or "The Lord" is our God and there is only one of Him. Moses clears their conscience and repairs any misconception, reminding them that the Lord is their God and that the Lord alone, is their God. There are no other gods, no other options, nor any lesser gods. There is no person, place, nor thing that should receive the treatment, reverence, or place of honor that belongs to God. Moses teaches them the name Yahweh, the most holy name for God. His name reminds us that God is faithful, merciful, gracious, patient, loving, truthful, forgiving, just, and righteous. God will be with you, to bless you, deliver you, and keep you. It doesn't matter where you are in life, how old you are or what you are doing when you encounter Him, the Lord is your God. Money does not make you. People cannot break you. Titles do not own you. The Lord is your God.

The Hebrews needed this word because the temptation for idol worship that was in Egypt was waiting for them at Mt. Sinai, and it would be waiting for them in the Promised Land as well. The temptation would arose again and they would have to fight against it again. So Moses stops to warn them ahead of time. They needed to get to know God, then love God, and begin to worship the Lord their God. They would do it through His commands (His word)!

In verse 5, Moses states that they shall love the Lord, their God. Delivered in a poetic prose, Moses then describes how to love the Lord, doing so with all your heart, soul and might. In verse 6, Moses instructs them to keep these words in their hearts. In verse 7, they're told to recite them to their children, talking about them when they are at home and away. Spatially, at home and away are extreme opposite of one another, implying that you are to talk about them all of the time, at home, away and in between. He also includes when you lie down and when you rise, suggesting that the family is together and that the child can learn about God when the families lie down together at night and when they rise together in the morning and prepare for the day. This gives the picture and impression that the family is together in unity and as the parents live out their faith, they are continually instructing their kids to live out theirs.

When Moses said, "Recite them to your children," the word recite means to teach, that is, to tell and explain all the laws and teachings recorded in Deuteronomy. The Message Bible translates this verse: "Get them inside of you and then get them inside your children."[xli] Also note the instruction that "the "Israelites were not to rely on public teaching but were to teach the commandments at home."[xlii] For members of this community raising children while discovering God for themselves, the uniqueness of the Shema rests within the timing of its delivery to both learn for themselves and to teach their children at the same time.

Who should teach at Home?

There have been many discussions on which parent is responsible for the spiritual direction of the children. Deuteronomy 6:7 gives us a clue. According to James Hamilton, "the verbs "you shall repeat" and "you shall talk" are second person masculine singular forms. Unlike English, which does not distinguish between masculine and feminine forms of the second person pronoun 'you,' Hebrew has a masculine and a feminine form for 'you.' The fact that these forms are masculine singular means that as Moses addresses the nation of Israel, he gives this responsibility to teach the sons directly to the fathers of those sons. The fact that the form is singular urges the conclusion that Moses is not giving this responsibility to some abstract group of fathers in the community but to each individual father."[xliii]

If the father is directly responsible for the spiritual direction of the children, in particular the sons, then what is the mother's responsibility? Ajith Fernando maintains that the mother's role is still vital: "Possibly the mother did the more systematic teaching that takes place in a routine manner, while the father's instruction focused more on the application of biblical truth to situations in the lives of the children, including their disciplining."[xliv] Ideally, both parents would be involved in giving the spiritual instruction to children.

What tools do Parents' Need?

Another topic of interest is the manner in which we communicate the commands to our children. In Deuteronomy 6:8-9, parents are instructed to "bind them as a sign on your hand, fix them as an emblem on your forehead, and write them on the doorposts of your house and on your gates" (NSRV). This is helpful to us as well. We're instructed to use whatever we can, to get the word at home. The signs on their hands are reminders to the individual, and the ones on the head are witnesses to others. If taken literally, perhaps the signs would reveal the commands through the senses to the consciousness of all as they were seen, remembered, and felt. James Hamilton taking this command figuratively, believes "the statements in Deuteronomy 6:8-9 are not to bring about some perfunctory activity of attaching the law to one's forehead or hand, doorpost or gates, because hands and eyes are figurative references to physical entities. Likewise, the doorposts and gates are to be marked by the word of God as a reflection of the inward reality that Israel is devoted to Yahweh."[xlv]

There is another argument that Moses' commands were meant to be taken literally, because this type of thing was regularly practiced in the ancient Near East at that time, [by] Israel's [pagan] neighbors [who] used it for their religious rituals."[xlvi] There is yet another argument to support taking this argument literally. Consider that since "books were few and scattered, they would write certain important parts of the law on their doorposts, bind them on their arms, and foreheads, and talk of them constantly.[xlvii]

The Israelites literally used phylacteries, "small black boxes,"[xlviii] or containers "made of the skin of clean animals, with four passages (Exodus 13:1–10; 13:11–16; Deuteronomy 6:4–9; 11:13) written by hand on parchment." They were attached to leather that were fastened to the left hand and the center of the forehead."[xlix] The phylactery, a transliteration of Greek phylaktērion, meaning 'a means of protection,'[l] "might have been viewed as apostrophic (i.e., protective). They were analogous to magical amulets known as qemia that were used in pagan circles."[li] For the Hebrews, they served as a reminder "that one was committed to obedience to the Torah. In Matthew's Gospel, Jesus criticized the Pharisees for wearing what he thought were oversized phylacteries as a way of flaunting their piety (23:5). He does not criticize the wearing of phylacteries in and of itself [though]."[lii]

The Israelites also attached small boxes with scripture in them to doorposts as a "challenge to remember always that the love of God is central to the faith." The "Mezuzah (Mě zū' zȧ) is the Hebrew term for "doorpost. Today mezuzah refers to small scrolls inscribed with Deuteronomy 6:4–9; 11:13–21 placed in a container attached to the doorjambs of some Jewish homes."[liii]

Parents today can learn a lot from the biblical command to teach our children. Since the Egyptians wore jewels on their forehead and arm, with inscriptions to protect them from danger, Moses took the jewelry, put scriptures on them and told his people to wear them. Then he told them to put the word on their doors, and on the gates of their homes as a witness to others but more importantly to put the word on the doors and gates of their hearts and minds. This text challenges us to stick to the orthodox attitude of submission to the scriptures, while challenging us to find new ways of communicating scripture."[liv]

The commands were placed on the person and on the person's possessions to symbolically show that the person and their belongings belong to God. In the same way that the Hebrews used cultural tools to socialize their beliefs, our young people today use music, jewelry, fashion, computers, social media and wearable technology to express their affiliation, and commitment to Christ. We should embrace their affection for these forms of expression and nurture them. The only question is will parents step up to the challenge.

God's Command to the Fathers

God has a special command to the fathers. Traditionally, Paul's call to parents in Ephesians to bring up their children in "the training and admonition of the Lord" (Ephesians 6:4),"[lv] and the Deuteronomy command in chapter 6 to "recite these commands to your children" have been identified as the Bible's key instructions to fathers on teaching children. You must note however that even before "Deuteronomy 6, God was preparing fathers in Israel to teach their children."[lvi] When Israelite fathers were taught to celebrate the Passover, they were instructed, "When your children ask you, 'What do you mean by this observance?' you shall say, 'It is the Passover sacrifice to the Lord, for he passed over the houses of the Israelites in Egypt, when he struck down the Egyptians but spared our houses.' When in the future your child asks you, 'What does this mean?' you shall answer, 'By strength of hand the Lord brought us out of Egypt, from the house of slavery" (Ex 12:26-27a, 13:14). This points to the observation that teaching was expected to begin at home, but it would also occur during special occasions and festivals, like the Passover.

As teachable moments abound, fathers are expected to instruct their children. As traditions are experienced, fathers are expected to train their children and correlate the significance of the experience to their God. Note that there are some generational benefits of teaching children in the family. God's "laws are passed from generation to generation," and history is preserved from generation to generation."[lvii] Again will fathers explain to their children the significance of what God has done in their lives? Will they stop and explain what God is doing now? Will they point to the future and give their children a vison of what God will do in their lives if they trust God?

The Deuteronomy 6:4-9 text provides some of God's final words spoken through Moses as the people were about to embark upon their own journey toward the fulfillment of God's promise. In the form of a treaty between God and man, they were taught to commit to God, to love Him, and to keep His word. As parents learned for themselves, they were instructed to teach their children, finding appropriate times and ways to teach their children at home, reminding themselves of the commands while being a witness to others. This points to the parents, in particular, the father's responsibility to teach his children about God. This must begin at home and the church must prepare the parents for this embarking.

Calling All Parents

I urge you parents, God is waiting for you to take the Word home with you! If you connect with your family and get the word into your hearts, God can do immeasurable, unthinkable things in your lives. The Lord is waiting for you. He's made His move. The next move is on you!

- If you don't know the Lord, He said, "I am the resurrection and the life. The one who believes in me will live, even though they die. (John 11:25)

- Once you know Him, remember He said, "I am the vine; you are the branches. If you remain in me and I in you, you will bear much fruit." (John 15:5a)

- To stay in Him, do as David. He said, "I have hidden your word in my heart that I might not sin against you." (Psalm 119:11)

- If you ever feel lost, remind Moses' words, "For the Lord your God goes with you; he will never leave you nor forsake you." (Deut 31:6b)

- Parents, trust Jesus and "Train up a child in the way he should go: and when he is old, he will not depart from it." (Proverbs 22:6b KJV)

- "Fathers, do not exasperate your children; instead, bring them up in the training and instruction of the Lord." (Ephesians 6:4 NIV)

- "Husbands, love your wives, even as Christ also loved the church, and gave himself for it; that he might sanctify & cleanse it with the washing of water by the word." (Eph. 5:25-26)

- Wives, submit yourselves unto your own husbands, as unto the Lord. (Eph. 5:22). Win them over by your behavior, "when they see the purity and reverence of your lives." (1 Peter 3:2b)

- Children, rise up each day, look at your mother and "Call her blessed" (Proverbs 31:28)

- Church, when God blesses you, take your testimony home with you. Jesus healed Legion, and told him "Go home to thy friends, and tell them [the] great things the Lord hath done for thee, and hath had compassion on thee. (Mark 5:19)

Other Benefits of Taking the Word Home

We discussed the biblical command to teach our children at home, but please also note that when you plant the seed of the Word into the hearts of your loved ones at home, you should expect to see growth. Children will remember the stories, lessons and scriptures you taught. Youth will ask hard questions that will make you open up your bible and search for the answers together. Couples will be yoked together by the spirit of God and will discover that a cord of three strands is not quickly broken. Parents will make disciples of their children. Young people will have enough word to fight the enemy with. Young adults will make better decisions in life. Women will build and nurture their relationships with each other. Men will get up and go get their own word at church. Our leaders will be led by God as they lead us. Officials will stand up for what is right rather than ignore what's wrong. People in power will bring forth justice to liberate the oppressed and restore people to wholeness. The body of Christ will come to church on fire. Then when bystanders, strangers and visitors witness the miraculous power in the church, they will ask, "What must I do to be saved?" Believers will put away their idols and focus on the sovereignty of Jesus Christ.

Discovery #3 - The Theologians Focused on the Family

The Early Church Fathers

Early church fathers placed much focus on the family. St. John Chrysostom in the fourth century agreed that parents should teach their own children. During the reformation, Martin Luther also wanted parents to aid in the spiritual foundation of their children. Modern scholars too are exploring methods of Christian education that either involves the parents.

This is important because parents can help children learn about God as they prepare to get to know who God is to them. This includes knowing God's attributes, His power to create and His authority over creation. They should learn of God's mercy and kindness to those who love and obey Him. Children must understand how God has been manifest in the three persons of the trinity so they will understand how they can expect to experience God as they grow. This is essential as they join the spiritual kingdom that the father God created, the Son of God rules, and the Spirit of God facilitates the activities of.

When God chooses to disclose Himself over the course of their lives, they will begin to grasp God's being (spiritual nature), Lordship, holiness, eternalness, and almightiness made available through the power of Christ (Christology) through the offering of Salvation (Soteriology). They will be brought into the knowledge of the Holy Scriptures which will one day make them wise, and able to understand and receive salvation through faith in Christ Jesus.

St. John Chrysostom

Let's look at the influence of the church fathers. St. John Chrysostom is considered "the greatest pulpit orator and commentator of the Greek Church."[lviii] He was significant in the era of the early church fathers and for "Eastern Orthodox communities of faith today."[lix] While responsible for "priestly and Episcopal responsibilities"[lx] during the late fourth century, in the "great urban centers of ancient Antioch and Constantinople,"[lxi] Chrysostom focused on the family lives of the flock. Chrysostom grew disappointed with the ethical carelessness and extreme obsession with wealth, leisure, social standing and obsession with their children's vocations, to the chagrin of their moral and spiritual growth. Chrysostom was compelled to address the functions of parents.

Chrysostom had a biblically inspired perception of parenthood, "deeply grounded in the Trinitarian and Christological teaching of the church."[lxii] He felt the child-parent relationship exemplifies those of the Trinity where the father and son reciprocate love through the Holy Spirit. Traditional Trinitarian teaching suggests that "God is self-revealed as triune, as threefold, named in the New Testament as Father, Son and Holy Spirit."[lxiii] Chrysostom's interpretation of the trinity translated into a family belief that "parents are called upon to emulate God the Father's love for his Son, while children should love and obey their parents the same way the Son loves and obeys the Father through the Spirit."[lxiv] I find that a novel idea and add that during bible reading time at home, parents should read the bible to learn how to love like the father and children should read to learn how to obey like son. Then they should compare notes.

Chrysostom firmly believed that families could imitate the triune love experienced between members of the Godhead. Family life not only mirrors the Godhead, it also mirrors the church. Chrysostom's Christological beliefs were "informed by the doctrine of imago Dei"[lxv] and led to his belief that all people including children were created in the image and likeness of God. Children however, relied on the effort of parents for God's work to be completed in them. Chrysostom views parents as "fellow workers with Christ (1 Cor 3:9), called to a transcendent, agape love where they will raise their children to the full stature of maturity in Christ (Eph 4:13; Col 1:28), as members of his body, the one holy, and apostolic church."[lxvi] He insists children learn through "instruction in the commandments, worship, the habit of prayer, and storytelling."[lxvii] If the family is like a church whose members live in the relational image of God, then parents must use it to train children to know God, for themselves. Together, the church and family must create the environment for them to learn and grow in Christ. Through the years, theologians focused on the family and we should do so today.

Theologians in the Middle Church Era

In the sixteenth century when Martin Luther sought to help parents raise mature, responsible children, he insisted parents "baptize their children, expose them to the Word and the sacraments, read the Bible with them, and pray with them."[lxviii] Luther wanted children to learn about the faith through oral teaching and through practical experience, believing that "faith comes only through God's grace and God's activity."[lxix] He was as concerned with their spiritual lives as well as their education. In fact, he wanted to impact the whole person even at an early age. Though Luther was not as "certain as Chrysostom before him or

Bushnell after him, he believed that a proper upbringing results in faith,"[lxx] and that "nurturing faith in children in large part is a result of the diligent work of parents, teachers, and other adults."[lxxi] I agree that we can impact the lives of children when the community works together. If the ministers, Christian educators, and primary educators work together, we can accomplish far more in the lives of our children.

More recent theologians contributed very little scholarship on the topic of children. We will therefore have to dig deeper into the wells of practical application and find new ways of communicating truths to our children. It was not until "the influential 1960 study by Philippe Aries, [that] a number of historians [began] directly exploring the history of childhood in the West."[lxxii] Theological discussion of children was not given serious consideration. It has been said that children are typically not considered when modern scholars discuss and debate the vital doctrines and beliefs of the faith and the Christian church.

Marcia Bunge believes there is a "lack in well-developed and historically and biblically informed teachings about children."[lxxiii] She believes the lack in both historical and contemporary theology is a contributing factor in the church's' struggle to establish and maintain ministry that acts as an advocate for children. There are conversations that may help us forge a way ahead. For example, contemporary theologian, Horace Bushnell, similar to Chrysostom, sees the family symbolically as a miniature church, which is the "primary agent of grace in the faith development of children, because religion never thoroughly penetrates life, until it becomes domestic."[lxxiv] I found this to be an important observation; for the child's spirit is formed naturally in the "daily routines and by interweaving lessons with play and fun activities."[lxxv] Today, we have to find ways to impart our faith and the

32

disciplines of our faith into our home lives. Later we will find that our customs as families were either influenced by God or were symbolic of the absence of God in our homes.

At home the family will teach the child to long for God, and to thirst for the word of God. Friedrich Daniel Ernst Schleiermacher, a Reformed theologian, believed that Christian families are appointed "to be the nurseries of the future generation, to train and develop them, and stir the earliest longings for fellowship with God."[lxxvi] At home, a child will hear the scriptures discussed, read and explained. The children will think about the scriptures and stories they hear. Children will ask questions about them and will inquire for deeper understandings. Schleiermacher suggests that at home children develop a living faith that is "something caught more than taught."[lxxvii] Parents must model faith for their children to see what it means to have faith in God.

Today's leaders and theologians would benefit by revisiting what takes place at home. Marcia Bunge suggests, "Congregational leaders have erred in allowing the focus of faith development to shift away from the family and to become centered in the congregation."[lxxviii] While researching methods of teaching children in the church, I deduced that today, we overlook the importance of the faith development that takes place at home. Bunge argues that "the family has the most potential of any institution for shaping the spiritual and moral lives of children; therefore, the best vehicles for the transmission of faith to children are family rituals, family service projects, and meaningful conversations with children in the home."[lxxix] I agree that the influence of the family on the child is central. For, if the family has the ability to scar children, and leave emotional baggage for decades, then they can make spiritual deposits that will produce fruit.

Discovery #4 - Theology must be taught

I set out to explore the theological pillars (or basic truths) of the faith, that underpin the urgent need for spiritual formation in children.

What is God like?

The first of these pillars is the theological question that asks what God is like. There is the belief that Spiritual formation begins with children understanding who God is and how God is. There is a foundational teaching and understanding that God exists and that God "may be known through both an affirmation of faith and an experience of faith."[lxxx] Before we experience Him, we should discover who God is. He is the source, creator, sustainer, and supplier of all and for all things. God's nature is "self-revealed in the scriptures, through the personal name, Yahweh, through the self-affirmation, I am who I am, which means I am the one that has being within myself (Ex. 3:14)."[lxxxi] God is "pure spirit, which means intelligent energy."[lxxxii] God is holy, "separate, and distinct;"[lxxxiii] God is Lord, which means "master, owner, and ruler."[lxxxiv] God is "infinite in time (eternity), in space (omnipresence), in knowledge (omniscience) and in power (omnipotence)."[lxxxv] God can be both transcendently apart from creation, yet immanently embodied within it. He walks with you through life even while He goes ahead to work things out for you.

What is Salvation (Soteriology)?

The second pillar is that we must understand salvation. In Introduction to Theology, Ellen Wondra writes, "salvation is always salvation for us (pro nobis) and, thus, must be presented in terms that address the actual situations in which persons find themselves."[lxxxvi] This is true for those of us who will introduce children to Christ. For children to understand that a real and present God is available to them, children must understand that God is available to help them in their unique situations where outcomes are made possible by way of God's intervention. Ellen Wondra adds that the doctrine of salvation can focus "narrowly on the significance of the death of Christ, somewhat more widely in the work of Christ, or most broadly in God's plan and will to bring the creation to its fulfillment."[lxxxvii] I find it imperative that for children to arrive at a decision for Christ they must understand the mere point that Jesus Christ died. Later as they develop an ongoing relationship with God, they must be taught from the broader perspective that there is salvation in the work of Christ. For it is God's plan to bring the whole creation to its fulfillment. We ultimately discern that everything Christ does is for our good.

V. A. Harvey suggests that there are "two basic perspectives in Christian history on the doctrine of salvation."[lxxxviii] One of them is "the Roman Catholicism and Eastern Orthodoxy perspective where salvation is understood as the participation of humanity in the divine life. It is sometimes called, in patristic theology, the deification of humanity, where for example, through the sacraments there is a theological emphasis on the incarnation of Christ."[lxxxix] The other is more characteristic of Protestantism where "salvation is understood as the restoration of a broken personal relationship, communion, and fellowship with God

35

through the forgiveness of sin primarily through preaching the word of divine favor and forgiveness. The theological language is that of personal existence, and the focus of theological emphasis is on the atonement of Christ."[xc]

Herbert W. Richardson suggests there is another theological perspective on salvation, from the American Protestant experience, that "the goal of creation is the sanctification of the world by the Holy Spirit, symbolized in the Sabbath. Since the divine holiness is incommunicable, God must personally enter the world in Christ."[xci] Some doctrines (e.g. trinity, incarnation) were defined because there was certain controversy over its definition. The church was therefore required to develop an "elaborately worked out synthesis,"[xcii] and come to an agreement on a doctrinal stance. Competitor schools debated the theology of Soteriology from the fourth to the twelfth century, "when Anselm's Cur dues homo (c. 1997) focused attention on it. A student seeking to understand Soteriology would have to pick his way through a variety of theories, that may have appeared unrelated and even mutually incompatible, existing side by side and sometimes sponsored by the same theologian."[xciii]

In addition to the theological perspectives on salvation, there are also three dominating themes related to the redemption offered through salvation. They "share a main theme, the ancient idea of recapitulation which Irenaeus derived from St. Paul, and which envisages Christ as the representative."[xciv] First, there is a "physical theory that sees the human nature of Christ as sanctified, transformed, and elevated by the incarnation."[xcv] A second theory, "traced to Irenaeus and Origen focuses on a ransom offered to the devil, or a more recent version where there is a forfeit is imposed on the devil."[xcvi] Lastly, there is a realist theory, where the cross is in the foreground. It is focused on the "Savior's sufferings for sin and the punishment due for it where Christ as substituting Himself for sinful men, shouldering the penalty which justice required for them to pay, and reconciling them to God by His sacrificial death."[xcvii]

Ambrose's theory is that Christ's death is a sacrifice, offered once and for all to satisfy the claims of divine justice where through Christ's blood, our sins are washed away. In Ambrose's view, Jesus took death upon Himself to satisfy the judgment that sinful flesh should be cursed even to unto death. In doing so, death and its sentence were destroyed, "when Jesus took flesh, abolished the curse of sinful flesh, and was made a curse in our place so the curse might be swallowed up in blessing."[xcviii] Pelagius agreed that God decreed death to sinners and added that Jesus Christ alone was "offered as a spotless sacrifice because, being innocent, He did not already deserve death on His own account."[xcix] "Jerome, too, although his ideas were unsystematic to a degree, recognized that Christ endured in our place and suffered the penalty we ought to have suffered for our crimes. No one, he claimed, can draw near to God apart from the blood of Christ."[c]

Whether you adopt a narrow or broader understanding of the salvific work of Jesus Christ, or whether you take the salvific perspective that deifies humanity or focuses on the atonement, you must be able to grasp and communicate the basic concept of salvation to your children. Whether you choose the physical, ransom or realist redemption themes you must understand and communicate the concept of redemption to you children, so they will understand the debt they owe to Jesus.

What is the Church (Ecclesiology)

The third theological pillar is the understanding of the church. The family and the larger, broader household, "played an important role in the development of early churches." [ci]The household included the parents, children, slaves, and other "dependents, such as servants, employees and even 'clients' (*e.g.* freedmen or friends) who voluntarily joined the household for mutual benefits." Many of the activities that lent to the formation of children occurred in the household, "e.g., the Passover meal, prayers, instruction, and fellowship."[cii] Children learned to read and write the alphabet and key scriptures in the home. They also started learning, very early. "As soon a boy could read, he received a scroll with Deuteronomy 6:4: 'Hear, O Israel: The Lord our God is one Lord'; for daily reciting, along with the Hallel (or psalm of praise), the story of creation, and the law. Teachings through Proverbs, parables, and an open sharing of knowledge occurred"[ciii] in the home. There was always questioning and answering taking place. Parents kept it simple, using "everyday illustrations and household objects to explain theological concepts."[civ] Early on, the family produced a learning environment for children to grow in. The family and extended family in the home was the first church for children.

What authority does Scripture have?

The final theological pillar is that the authority of scripture must be understood. If you look back to the early church's history, you will see the challenge to the church's stance on the authority of scripture.

There are invaluable writings that give a glimpse into the "life and community of the church or into the lack of it."[cv] It appears there was a persistent and consistent threat to the authority of scripture and to the Christian community itself. These writings include Irenaeus' writing in the second century A.D., Cyprian's writing in a time of persecution and martyrdom in the middle of the third century, and Augustine's writing in the later fourth and early fifth centuries.

Father Irenaeus, Bishop of Lyon, faced the Gnostic threat in the second century A.D. There were a variety of Gnostic teachers (e.g. Marcion, Basilides, Carpocrates, Cerinthus and Valentinus) who taught that "creation was the act, not of God the Father, but rather of the Demiurge, either a wicked angel or a lesser deity."[cvi] This challenged our belief that God alone is the source, creator, sustainer, and supplier of all for all things. The Gnostics also argued "that a lesser deity-the Demiurge-was responsible for inspiring the Old Testament."[cvii] This was an attempt to weaken the authority of the Old Testament. The Gnostics also created their own canon by writing their own sacred documents and by modifying New Testament documents. The Gnostics both challenged the church's core beliefs about origin and authority of scripture. Reading this helps us understand that the church needed to understand the core truths regarding scripture and then communicate their beliefs publicly.

Irenaeus responded to the Gnostics' challenge to the bible and to the use of divine revelation by proclaiming that Scripture has authority because it is inspired and communicated by God. He argued that after Jesus died, the apostles received power, gifts and knowledge from the Holy Spirit. The resulting revelation, interpretation and testimony are divinely inspired and set apart as the word of God. The apostles "traveled throughout the Mediterranean basin, bearing witness to Christ both orally and in written form."[cviii] While the Gnostics relied on secret revelation and believed their secret revelation was more trustworthy than the scriptures, Irenaeus and others like him suggest they look no further than the apostles of Christ for revelation. They stood on the apostolic testimony of the church. They found true knowledge in the narrative of the Scriptures that were passed on and authoritatively interpreted by the prophets, Jesus and the apostles, faithfully preserved by the bishops of the church. Today, we must continue to stand on the authority of scripture and use the word of God to guide our lives. As we lead our households, as the primary facilitators of faith development, we parents must use scripture in a form that our children can understand, remember, and apply for their long term growth

Conclusion

In conclusion parents, I urge you that there is an urgent need to teach our children. I've discovered a formidable method that's existed for millennia that can help us. This method is the catechism and it suggests that we first figure out what we want our children to learn. Then we will teach them the answers, and test them with the questions. Since we have a biblical mandate to teach our children throughout the day, you should use everything in sight. I insist that you become dynamic leaders in the home. Give your children layers of foundation. Ask the hard questions to help them wrestle with the great concepts of our faith. Use everything available as teaching tools. Life is full of objects and lessons. Your children are waiting with questions and they need your guidance.

They need deserve tangible, relative thoughts to wrestle with. They need more supportive scripture to chew on, and contemplations from historical and contemporary figures to reflect on. Dr. Tom Boomershine, a leader in Biblical Storytelling, shared his thoughts with me on biblical storytelling and its implications for children. We agreed that our children should be geared toward learning the details of the bible's stories, memorization of the stories, retelling the stories, and enacting the stories. Our youth should be able to answer some of the difficult questions of the sacred texts. They should be able to relate to the difficult decisions made in scripture and deduce how they will handle similar situations in their own lives.

Lastly, I believe the church will work collaboratively with parents to find more practical ways to teach children. They will learn the commands of God. They will remember them when they awake each day, remember how to live for God throughout the day, and then reflect again at night for assurance that they've lived accordingly.

There's a more practical way to address the need for parental involvement. The church should help parents talk about the commands when they are at home and when away. We can use today's film, animation, internet, devices, and television to provide and communicate lessons for us. Even more, fathers can step up and take the lead. To facilitate this, I recommend the Journey of Faith Study Guide. It was designed using a unique curriculum designed for children, youth and adults to learn biblically, theologically and practically. It features:

- Biblical stories and texts for family reading time
- A Devotional to inspire adults and edify them in the faith
- Adult Self Reflection questions
- Adult Journal (to write to share your thoughts)
- A Prophetic Point (1 phrase short summary)
- A Youth Catechism to teach the biblical and theological truths
- A Children's Chat, to help them retell the details of the story
- A prayer or poem for the family to share
- A parent tip for reinforcing the lesson at home
- An answer key for the children and youth lessons

BIBLIOGRAPHY

Bauerlein, Mark. The Digital Divide: Arguments for and Against Facebook, Google, Texting, and the Age of Social Networking. September, 2011.

Brand, C. Draper, C. England, A. Bond, S. Clendenen, E. R. and Butler, T. C. Mezuzah. Holman Illustrated Bible Dictionary. Nashville, TN, Holman Bible Publishers, 2003.

Brown, David, Fausset, A. R., Jamieson, R. Commentary Critical and Explanatory on the Whole Bible. Oak Harbor, WA, Logos Research Systems Inc., 1997.

Children's Ministry International, Inc. www.childministry.com/about.htm. Tucker, Georgia 30084-4499.

Clark, Steve. Parents' teaching, Research Brief: Intentional Fathering, Adapted From Steve Clark, "Intentional Fathering: Fathers' Positive Influence on the Relational Spiritual Formation of Their Children." Ed. D. diss., Talbot School of Theology, 2011.

Cranton, Patricia. *Professional Development as Transformative Learning: New Perspectives For Teachers of Adults.* 1st edition. San Francisco, CA: Jossey-Bass, 1996.

Douglas Vos. The Aquila Report. www.theaquilareport.com/the-basics-of-the-bible-a-curriculum-for-children. Reformed Churchmen Publications, Inc., Erie, CO 80516-1164.

Doing Church History: A User-Friendly Introduction to Researching the History of Christianity.

Dyson, Michael Eric. Is Bill Cosby Right? *Reprinted by arrangement with Basic Civitas, a member of the Perseus Books Group. http://www.npr.org /templates/story/story.php?storyId=4628960.*

Ellison, H. L. *New Bible Dictionary.* 3rd ed. Downers Grove, IL: InterVarsity Press, 1996.

Evangelical Presbyterian Church. Office of the General Assembly. http://www.epc.org/ministries/cec/childrens-curriculum. Livonia, MI 48152-7912.

Fernando, Ajith. Preaching the Word, Deuteronomy, Loving Obedience to a Loving God, Wheaton, IL: Crossway, 2012.

Fuhrmann, Justin M. *Journal of the Evangelical Theological Society,* Deuteronomy 6-8 and the History of Interpretation: An Exposition on the First Two Commandments, vol. 53, no. 1, March 2010.

Glatt-Gilad, D. A., and Powell, M. A. Phylacteries, *The Harper Collins Bible Dictionary* 3rd Ed. New York, NY: Harper Collins, 2011.

Great Commission Publications, Inc. www.gcp. Suwanee, GA, 30024-3897. Sixth Printing, 2009.

Hall, Christopher A. *Learning Theology with the Church Fathers.* 2002

Halley, Henry Hampton. *Halley's Bible Handbook,* NIV. Grand Rapids, MI: Zondervan Publishing House, 2000.

Hamilton, James M. Jr. http://www.sbts.edu/family/blog/that-the-coming-generation-might-praise-the-lord-by-james-m-hamilton, "Family Ministry Today, That the Coming Generation Might Praise the Lord," *The Center for Christian Family Ministry*, The Southern Baptist Theological Seminary, Accessed April 20, 2013.

Haynes, Brian. "Helping Parents Lead Their Children Biblically, http://www. Faithformation2020.net/uploads/5/1/6/4/5164069/helping_parents_l ead_their_children_biblically_-_haynes.pdf, K! Magazine.

Hunt, Richie; Hunt Susan. Big Truths for Little Kids: Teaching Your Children to Live for God, Rossway, 1999.

Johnson, Luke T. *The Anchor Bible*: The First and Second Letters to Timothy, Garden City, NY: Doubleday, 1964.

Katt, Arthur F. "From a Child Thou Hast Known the Holy Scriptures," (2 Tim. 3:15), Teach So Kids Understand, *Concordia Theological Monthly* 25, 1954.

Klutterman, David. LeaderResources, LLC. **The Catechism Curriculum.** http:// leaderresources.org/catechism-curriculum. Leeds, MA 01053-0302.

Krych, Margaret A. "Toward a 21st Century Catechism. Structuring the Catechism," Lutheran Theological Seminary at Philadelphia.

Lange, J. P, Schaff, P., & Van Oosterzee, J. J. A Commentary on the Holy
Scriptures: 1 & 2 Timothy, Bellingham, WA, Logos Bible Software,
2008.

Laurro, Ben. *2014 Gospel Light.* www.gospellight.com/content.aspx?id=121.
Pure Publicity. *Ventura, CA 93003.*

Lockman, Vic. Doorposts. http://www.doorposts.com/details.aspx?id=7.
Gaston, OR 97119.

McDonald, William P. *Methodist Catechisms, What Shall We Do For The Rising
Generation,* 1745-1934.

Mish, Frederick C. http://biblia.com/books/mwdict11/offset/2758291,
Catechize, Shared from Logos Bible Software, http://www.logos.com,
Merriam-Webster's Collegiate Dictionary, 11th Edition by
Merriam-
Webster, Apr 23, 2008.

Mitchell, Christine. http://touchstonejournal.ca/pdf/23_1_2005.pdf, Heart and
Mind in the Hebrew Scriptures, *Touchstone Journal,* vol. 23, no. 1,
January, 2005 Accessed April 20, 2013.

Nelson, Ellis. "Spiritual Formation: A Family Matter," *Family Ministry,* vol. 20
no. 3, Fall 2006.

New Psalmist Baptist Church, New Psalmist Baptist Church, Male Mentorship
Ministry Plan.

Pickett, Kate. Wilkinson, Richard. *The Spirit Level: Why Greater Equality Makes
Societies Stronger.*

Piper, John. The Baptist Catechism. Revised version of "The Baptist Catechism.
The Philadelphia Baptist Association (1742). www.desiringGod.org.
1986.

Presbyterian Church (U.S.A.). Belonging to God: A First Catechism with
Biblical References. Approved by the 210th General Assembly (1998)
of the Presbyterian Church (U.S.A.).
www.pcusa.org/resource/belonging-god-first-catechism-biblical-
references. Louisville, KY: 40202.

Ray, Teddy. Why United Methodists should have a catechism, originally *from* http://www.seedbed.com. www.unitedmethodistreporter.com/2012/08/why-united-methodists-should-have-a-catechism, *Asbury Theological Seminary,* 2012.

Roberts, Dianne L. New Psalmist Baptist Church, Kingdom Kidz Discipleship 2012-2013 Handbook.

Schaff, P., & Schaff, D. S., Chapter VI. Propagation and Persecution, (1910), History of the Christian church. http://biblia.com/books/schaff/offset/13769483, Shared from Logos Bible Software http://www.logos.com, New York, NY: Charles Scribner's Sons.

Schaff, Philip. *History of the Christian Church, Apostolic Christianity,* vol. 1., Wm. B. Erdmans Publishing Company, Grand Rapids, MI: 1910, By Charles Scribner's Sons, Copyright in electronic form 1996, by Historical Exegetical 'Lectronic Publishing (HE'LP), Saginaw, MI.

Stone, Dave. Faithful Families series, Families are a key, Excerpted from Ministry Matters.com, http://www.ministrymatters.com/all/article/entry/2802/families-are-key-to-the-future-of-the-church#ixzz2KR1L1QJa, Accessed April 20, 2013.

Taggar-Cohen, Ada. Biblical Covenant and Hittite ishiul Reexamined, VT 61.3, Doshisha University, Kyoto, 2011.

Thomas Nelson Publishers. The Holy Bible: New Revised Standard Version. 2 Ti 3:2–5. Nashville, Thomas Nelson Publishers, 1989.

Towns, Elmer L. Wesley on Religious Education, John Wesley and Religious Educations, Associate Professor of Christian Education, Trinity Evangelical, Divinity School, Deerfield, IL.

Trost, Frederick R. The Evangelical Catechism, Louis Edward Nollau and the "Evangelical Catechism," an address delivered at Eden Theological Seminary, November 6, 2010.

Watts, James W. *Reading Law: The Rhetorical Shaping of the Pentateuch.* Sheffield: Sheffield Academic, 1999.

Weinfeld, Moshe. Deuteronomy 1-11. New York, NY: Doubleday, 1991.

Willmington, H. L. *The Outline Bible*. Wheaton, IL: Tyndale House, Jan 28, 2000.

Wondra, Ellen K. *Introduction to Theology*, 3rd Edition. Morehouse Publishing. 2002.

Wright, David F. "A Family Faith: Domestic Discipling." *Bibliotheca Sacra*, July -September 2003: 160.

ENDNOTES

[i] _____. s.v., "oral instruction."

[ii] Merriam-Webster, s.v., "religious doctrine," *Merriam-Webster's Collegiate Dictionary*. Springfield, MA: Merriam-Webster, Inc. 2003.

[iii] _____. s.v., "catechism."

[iv] _____. s.v., "resound."

[v] Merrian Webster, "Repetition," accessed March 3, 2014, http://www.merriam-webster. com/ dictionary/din.

[vi] The Free Dictionary, "Hammer into," accessed March 3, 2014, http:// idioms. Thefreedicti onary.com/din+into.

[vii] Rieger

[viii] Margaret A. Krych, Toward a 21st Century Catechism, Structuring the Catechism (Philadelphia PA: Lutheran Theological Seminary at Philadelphia).

[ix] Ibid.

[x] Ibid.

[xi] P. Schaff, & D. S. Schaff, Chapter VI. Propagation and Persecution, (1910), History of the Christian church. http://biblia.com/books/schaff/offset/13769483, Shared from Logos Bible Software http://www.logos.com, New York: Charles Scribner's Sons.

[xii] Teddy Ray, "Why United Methodist Should Have a Catechism," August 30, 2012, http://www.united methodistreporter.com/2012/08/why-united-methodists-should-have-a-catechism, Why United Methodists should have a catechism, originally *from http://www.* seedbed.com, *Asbury Theological Seminary.*

[xiii] Ibid.

[xiv] William P McDonald, *Methodist Catechisms, What shall we do for the rising generation, 1745-1934.*

[xv] Elmer L. Towns, *Wesley on Religious Education, John Wesley And Religious Educations* (Deerfield, IL: Trinity Evangelical, Divinity School).

[xvi] Towns, *Wesley on Religious Education,* 7.

[xvii] Ibid.

[xviii] Ibid., 4.

[xix] Towns

[xx] Daniel G. Reid, Robert Dean Linder, Bruce L. Shelley, and Stout Harry S., accessed April 16, 2013, http://biblia.com/books/dca/offset/1242688, Dictionary of Christianity in America. Catechetics, Catholic, Shared from Logos Bible Software http://www.logos.com, Downers Grove, IL: Intervarsity, 1990.

[xxi] Ibid.

[xxii] Margaret A. Krych, *Toward a 21st Century Catechism. Structuring the Catechism,* (Philadelphia, PA: Lutheran Theological Seminary at Philadelphia).

[xxiii] Ibid., 2.

[xxiv] Ibid., 6.

[xxv] Steve Clark, Parents' Teaching, Research Brief: Intentional Fathering, Adapted from

Steve Clark, "Intentional Fathering: Fathers' Positive Influence on the Relational Spiritual Formation of Their Children" (Ed. D. diss., Talbot School of Theology, 2011).

[xxvi]David F. Wright, "A Family Faith: Domestic Discipling," *Bibliotheca Sacra 160,* July-September 2003.

[xxvii]McDonald, "Methodist Catechisms," 14.

[xxviii]D. R. W. Wood, Marchall, I. Howard, *The New Bible Dictionary*, Third Edition (Downers Grove, IL: InterVarsity Press, December 9, 1996), 893.

[xxix]James W. Watts, *Reading Law: The Rhetorical Shaping of the Pentateuch* (Sheffield, UK: Sheffield Academic, 1999), 116.

[xxx]H. L. Willmington, *The Outline Bible* (Wheaton, IL: Tyndale House, Jan 28, 2000), 51.

[xxxi]Ajith Fernando, *Preaching The Word, Deuteronomy, Loving Obedience to a Loving God* (Wheaton, IL: Crossway, 2012), 26.

[xxxii]Justin M. Fuhrmann, "Deuteronomy 6-8 and the History of Interpretation: An Exposition on the First Two Commandments," *Journal of the Evangelical Theological Society,* vol. 53, no. 1, March 2010: 37.

[xxxiii]Willmington, *The Outline Bible,* 51.

[xxxiv]Willmington, *The Outline Bible,* 52.

[xxxv]Taggar-Cohen, "Biblical Covenant and Hittite ishiul Reexamined," 7.

[xxxvi]Ibid.

[xxxvii]James M. Hamilton, Jr., accessed April 20, 2013, http://www.sbts.edu/family/blog/that-the-coming-generation-might-praise-the-lord-by-james-m-hamilton, Family Ministry Today, That the Coming Generation Might Praise the Lord, The Center for Christian Family Ministry, The Southern Baptist Theological Seminary, 2013, 11.

[xxxviii]Ellis Nelson, "Spiritual Formation: A Family Matter," *Family Ministry,* vol. 20, no. 3, Fall 2006: 13.

[xxxix]Ibid., 14.

[xl]Ibid.

[xli]Ibid., 19.

[xlii]Ibid.

[xliii]Hamilton, "Family Ministry Today," 12.

[xliv]Fernando, *"Preaching the Word,"* 254.

[xlv]Hamilton, "Family Ministry Today," 13.

[xlvi]Fernando, *Preaching the Word,* 268.

[xlvii]Henry Hampton Halley, *Halley's Bible Handbook with the New International Version* (Grand Rapids, MI: Zondervan Publishing House, 2000), 177.

[xlviii]D. A. Glatt-Gilad and M. A. Powell, "Phylacteries," *The Harper Collins Bible Dictionary,* Third Edition (New York, NY: Harper Collins, 2011), 804–805.

[xlix]H. L. Ellison, "Phylacteries," *New Bible Dictionary*. 3rd ed. (Downers Grove, IL: InterVarsity Press, 1996), 927.

[l]Ibid.

[li]Glatt-Gilad, "Phylacteries," 804.

[lii]Ibid.

[liii]Ibid., 805.

[liv]Fernando, *Preaching The Word,* 254.

[lv]Dave Stone, Faithful Families Series, Families are a key, Excerpted from MinistryMatters.com, http://www.ministrymatters.com/all/article/entry/2802/families-are-key-to-the-future-of-the-church#ixzz2KR1L1QJa.

[lvi]Hamilton, "Family Ministry Today," 11.

[lvii]Stone, "Faithful Families Series," 1.

[lviii]John Chrysostom, Philip Schaff, George Barker Stevens, John Albert Broadus, *The Complete Works of Saint John Chrysostom* (33 Books with Active Table of Contents), Oct 24, 2011.

[lix]Marcia J Bunge, *The Child in Christian Thought* (Grand Rapids, MI: Wm. B. Eerdmans Publishing Company, 2001).

[lx]Ibid., 21.

[lxi]Ibid., 63.

[lxii]Ibid., 64.

[lxiii]Ellen K. Wondra, *Introduction to Theology*, 3rd Edition (Atlanta, GA: Morehouse Publishing, July 1, 2002).

[lxiv]Bunge, *The Child in Christian Thought,* 64.

[lxv]Ibid.

[lxvi]Ibid., 75.

[lxvii]Ibid.

[lxviii]Ibid., 21.

[lxix]Ibid.

[lxx]Ibid.

[lxxi]Ibid.

[lxxii]Ibid., 2.

[lxxiii]Ibid.

[lxxiv]Bunge, *The Child in Christian Thought,* 22.

[lxxv]Ibid., 23.

[lxxvi]Ibid., 98.

[lxxvii]Ibid., 20.

[lxxviii]Ibid.

[lxxix]Ibid.

[lxxx]Wood & Marshall, *New Bible Dictionary*, 417.

[lxxxi]Ibid.

[lxxxii] Wondra, *Introduction to Theology*, location 1958.

[lxxxiii]Ibid., location 1958.

[lxxxiv]Ibid., location 1865.

[lxxxv]Wood & Marshall, *New Bible* Dictionary, 419.

[lxxxvi]Wondra, Introduction to Theology, location 3518.

[lxxxvii]Ibid.

[lxxxviii]Ibid., location 3526.

[lxxxix]Ibid.

[xc]Ibid.

[xci]Ibid., location 3527.

[xcii]Ibid.

[xciii]H. Kraft, *Early Christian Thinkers* (Downers Grove, IL: Intervarsity Press, 2010).

[xciv]Ibid., 376.

[xcv]Ibid., 375.

[xcvi]Ibid.

[xcvii]Ibid.

[xcviii]Ibid., 389.

[xcix]Ibid., 389.

[c]Ibid.

[ci] Wood & Marshall, *New Bible Dictionary*, 202.

[cii]Ibid., 363.

[ciii]W. A. Elwell & B. J. Beitzel, *Baker Encyclopedia of the Bible* (Grand Rapids, MI: Baker Book House), 988.

[civ]C. Ryrie, *Ryrie's Practical Guide to Communicating Bible Doctrine* (Nashville, TN: Broadman & Holman Publishers, 2005).

[cv]Christopher A Hall, Learning Theology with the Church Fathers, e-book location 2883.

[cvi]Ibid., location 2820.

[cvii]Ibid., location 2584.

[cviii]Ibid., location 2591.

Journey of Faith Ministries

ABOUT THE AUTHOR

Dr. Derrick L Randolph, Sr. is from Baltimore, Maryland.